CONTENTS

Jordan has been the stage of continuous inhabitation for more than ten millenniums. It has a large share of the events mentioned in both the Bible and the Quran, adding more to its geographical, historical and cultural values.

The Rose Finch, national bird of Jordan

Situated in the west of Asia forming a link with the north of Africa through the Sinai desert, geographically Jordan is the southern part of what's known as *Greater Syria* and the north of the *Arabian Desert*. The significant position of this region was the reason for many states and communities to settle and benefit from. Perhaps the most fascinating story of all is the one connected with the *Nabataean Petra,* or *Metropolis Arabia* as the Romans called it.

Traces of prehistoric periods have been and are still being revealed. Some of the first settlements of the first agricultural communities thrived here. As acknowledged by archaeologists; these were the first sparks of civilizations stretching along the *Fertile Crescent* making the first steps towards the progress of mankind. This all became possible after the decline of the *Ice Age* some 13,000 years ago, and the good climate conditions within the region; allowing many kinds of the known domesticated animals to find a convenient habitat. This abundance was the fuel for inventions and creations by man.

The possibility of linking to Africa, Europe and the Mediterranean from the west, and India, China and Persia from the east made the region a stage for rivalries between great nations existing here. The Babylonians, Assyrians, Pharaohs of Egypt, Greeks and the Romans, all tried to have a foothold here; the reason was clear and logic, it's the flow of merchandise and caravans routes through all directions, taxes and duties collected by states were major attributes of existence, and the result, hundreds and even thousands of places and landmarks of historical value, established by various periods and cultures in the region. Many of the sites in Jordan are listed in the UNESCO World Heritage sites such as Petra, Amra bath complex and the Baptism site on The Jordan.

According to the recent venture of the New Seven Wonders of the world (7th July 2007), Petra was elected second and recognized as a wonder in the new millennium. And it is the most visited site in all of Jordan.

The new state represents an ambitious community with a modern leadership of the ruling dynasty of the Hashemites, headed by King Abdullah bin Al Husain II, the head of the 43rd generation of the dynasty descending from the Prophet Muhammad.

King Abdullah II of Jordan

Jordan still benefits from its location as a transit country for the surrounding neighbors, and is a major producer of Phosphates and Potash products.

In the last decade the country achieved major leaps in economy; the experience of Free Zones, joint investments and designation of new tourist destinations and latest archaeological discoveries gave thrust to the overall development process, regardless of the extreme geopolitical and humanitarian conditions of the Mid-Eastern region connected with the Arab-Israeli conflict and the invasion of Iraq by the US and its allies.

Until recent years, Jordan wasn't the most visited destination of the region compared to Egypt or others, but it undoubtedly has many features to surprise any visitor from around the globe, and numbers of inbound tourists are increasing year by year.

After signing the Araba document between Jordan and Israel in 1994, Jordan became a key player in the tourist itineraries through the Middle East, and a week or so spent in this historically rich country is a worthwhile experience to have; from the classical cities and religious places, to adventure and eco-tourism, the country is well facilitated to fulfill as much of the needs of its visitors with a rather inexpensive budget compared to other well known destinations around the world.

THE HASHEMITE KINGDOM
OF JORDAN

Territory	92,300 km^2 = 35,637 sq mi.
Population	2009 estimate 6,316,000. The majority are Arabs, and also Armenians, Syrians, Chechens, Circassians, Turks and Kurds.
Capital city	Amman 31°57′N 35°56′E.
Ruling system	Constitutional monarchy with an elected parliament every four years. The head of state is king Abdullah bin Al Hussein II (since 1999).
Demonym	Jordanian.
Religion	Sunni Muslims 92% Christian 6% *(Greek Orthodox and Catholics).*
Time zone	GMT +2
Currency	The Jordanian Dinar= JD= 100 piaster or qirsh. *(1 USD = 0.708 JD).*
language	Arabic. English is spoken in major cities and tourist locations.
Climate	Generally Mediterranean, subtropical in the Jordan valley and the south. Average temperatures: Winter 15°C = 59°F, Summer 35°C = 95°F.
Working hours	State offices 8:00 -15:00, Banks 9:00-15:00 from Sunday to Thursday. Friday and Saturday are the week holidays.
Measurements	Metric system is widely used.
Electricity	220 v-50Hz.
GDP (nominal)	2008 estimate, Total $21.225 billion, Per capita $3,776
Calling code	962
Internet TLD	.jo
Independence	25 May 1946.

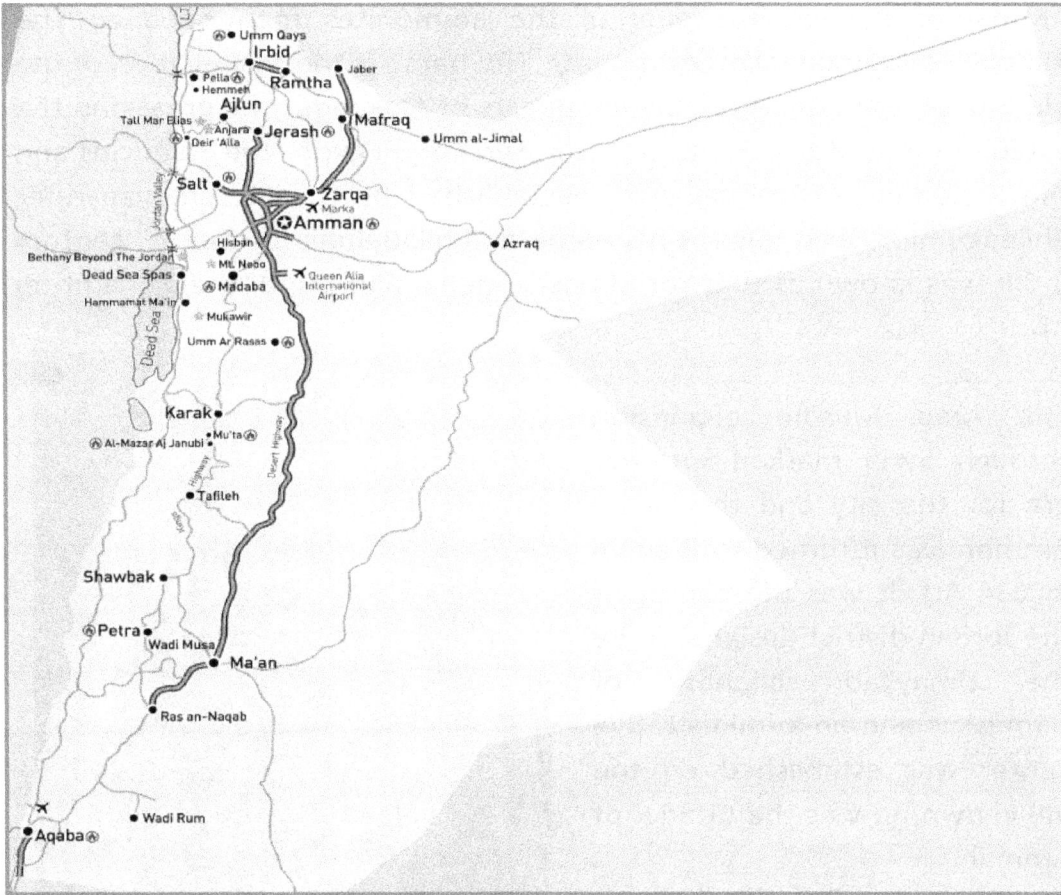

The flag of the Hashemite Kingdom of Jordan

The colors of the flag indicate the different Islamic periods that passed over the region:

The red color and the star refer to The Hashemites 1515-1520 AD.
White refers to the Umayyads 661-750 AD.
Black refers to the Abbasids 750-1258 AD.
Green refers to the Fatimids 908-1171 AD.

Amman, the ancient capital of the ammonites mentioned as The Rabbah of Ammon *(Old Testament).* The name is the assimilation of the old Biblical Ammon. After the conquests of Alexander the great and the establishment of the Greek states in Syria and Egypt –the Seleucids and the Ptolemeyan- Amman was reestablished by the Ptolemeyan ruler Philadelphius, who gave it his name as Philadelphia in the 3rd century B.C.It was known as that for almost a millennium until the 7th century AD.

The Arab Muslim expansion through Syria marked another era for the city and the name Ammon was returned to it again in 634 AD. It was the center of the Jordan district designated by the Umayyad caliphate of Damascus and an administrative center was established on the hill known now as the Citadel of Amman.

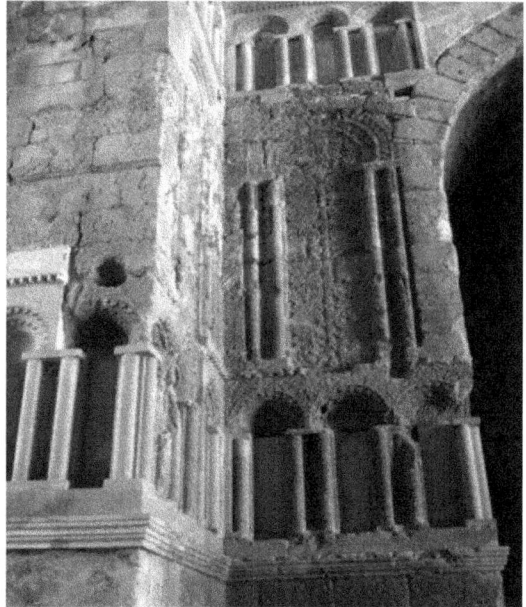

The familiar Islamic art in The Vestibule of the Umayyad palace

The remains of the Hercules temple were restored recently standing now as the historical symbol of the city. It dates back to the 2nd c. at a time when it was counted as one of the famous Decapolis cities of eastern Rome. Archaeological surveys revealed the magnitude of this classical site once thrived as a commercial station on the ancient trade routes.

The hills of Amman in the background of the Temple of Hercules

The city plays a vital role in the modern Jordanian life; the centered location between different parts of the country makes it easy to connect with. Several bus stations are located around the city with destinations to all major cities around in addition to two international airports, the yellow taxi service is also available 24/7.

Local Jordanian cuisine is also well known, a wide choice of restaurants and diners is available including traditional local and continental menus, and trying the local dish Mansaf (boiled lamb in yoghurt served with rice) would be a good choice.

Places recommended to visit:

The Citadel
The Roman Theater (including museums)
The Down Town area (King Talal STR.)
The Archaeological Museum of Jordan
King Abdullah I Mosque
The Wild Jordan facility of *The Royal Society for the Conservation of Nature.*
The Rainbow str.
The Royal Automobile Museum

The Roman Theater

and the Odeon

A view of Amman

King Abdullah I
mosque in Amman

Jerash is one of the best classical Roman provincial cities in the world, it's known also as Pompey of the east; the preservation level is outstanding and it is the second item on tourist itineraries. The city of **Antioch on The Golden River** –the first Greek name of the site-, was established around the 3rd century BC.

After the conquests of Alexander the Great, the region entered what is commonly called the Hellenistic era 332 BC. The new culture emerged with the local Aramaic communities and produced a chain of metropolises that were later named as The Decapolis, a union of ten or more cities of the Graeco-Roman era (332 BC – 335 AD) in which Jerash was a key player.

The first ever known name of the place was Garshu or the Roman Gerasa that assimilated finally into Jerash.

The Gate of Hadrian, 130 AD.

As you enter through the Hadrian Gate which is the southern side of the ruins, the remains of the Gerasa Circus stand on the left, this was a place for some 15,000 people that watched the traditional Roman shows of gladiators and chariot races almost every day. This facility entertained the citizens of Gerasa and the surrounding area, and the shows were sponsored by the elite.

The Gerasa Circus

The actual boundaries of the city at the time where beyond the circus; the walls of the ruins start at the Philadelphia Gate, or as others call it the Southern Gate, a smaller copy of the Hadrian Gate.

As you pass the gate into the city, the track leads you to one of the defining moments of the site; The Forum of Jerash, this was -according to archaeological surveys- the original beginning of the Greek city established in the 3rd century BC., including the hill accommodating the Zeus Temple and the opposite hill, where the Archaeological Museum is situated.

The Forum of Jerash

The remains of the Temple of Zeus Opposite the Forum. Much of the damage is referred to numerous earthquakes that hit the region in past centuries; the most influential was the 750 AD. When the city was abandoned in the Muslim Umayyad era

The city entered the Roman era with the conquests of General Pompey in the year 63 BC. The 2nd and 3rd centuries were the golden years of the Decapolis era in Jordan; and metropolises were established and reestablished marking the region with the Hellenistic style and affecting the existing cultures.

General Pompey

In the new era, and after being abandoned and forgotten for centuries, a German traveler, Ulrich Seetsen, discovers the city with the thousand colonnades of Gersa.

Most of the site was under layers of dust and rubble with columns standing through different spots of the city. Restoration and surveys were held in the 20th century by the Department of Archaeology of Jordan and different world wide institutions and organizations.

The Cardo

The South Theater

The North Theater

The entrance to the Macella

Temple of Artemis

Pillars of the Artemis Temple

Um Qais or Biblical *Gadara,* another Hellenistic site and a member of the Decapolis Classical cities. Situated in the north of Jordan over viewing Lake Tiberius, The Jordan Valley and the Golan Heights of Syria, Surrounded with lush hills of forests and olive plantations the city served as a leisure and relaxation area; especially with the abundance of the natural hot springs lying on both sides of the Yarmouk Gorge separating Syria from Jordan.

The site is close to the famous Yarmouk Battle site 634AD. In which the Muslims marked a new era of the region, eliminating the influence of Byzantium and expanding to the borders of Turkey.

Historically the area is very well known even before the Biblical times; tens of prehistoric sites were revealed around and archaeological surveys proved that some of the earliest inhabitation sites in the Middle East were established here. The site is famous for it's black basalt structure; since this was an ancient volcanic activity area that formed the plateau on the north-west of the country.

The original town of Um Qais is situated on the eastern side of Gadara, embracing the theater and edging with what is now the rest house. In many of these houses stone fragments from ancient Gadara are used especially on entrances and window lentils. The museum house contains a good variety of sculptures, artifacts and mosaics related to the area.

Tomb fragments

Basalt stone tomb entrance

After the death of Alexander the Great in 323 BC. The city was established by the Ptolemies; who rivaled with their neighbors, the Seleucids of Syria. Each was trying to have a foot hold in the region. Gadara switched from one hand to another until the roman order was established after the conquests of Gen. Pompey of Rome. The city became a member of the Decapolis chain with autonomous rule.

This was firmly common after the take over of Petra in 106 AD. By Trajan who established a network of roads and connections through the region which later became famous as *Via Nova Trajana,* or the *Kings Highway* which was the connection between the ancient Biblical kingdoms of *Edom, Moab* and *Ammon.*

The place flourished in the 2nd century as a resort area and a place for philosophers, poets and performing artists; some common names of that period are associated with Gadara like *Menippos, Meleager, Theodoros of Gadara* and others.

The Colonnaded street of Gadara

Gadara is also very well known for its Biblical reference with the story of Jesus Christ crossing the Sea of Galilee and healing the insane man in Gadara .

The shops of Gadara underneath the Octagonal Church

In the 4th century the city was the seat of a bishopric, but this was for a short period; the decisive battles of Tabaqat Fahl- *Pella,* and Yarmouk in 634 AD., put the city in the hands of he new Muslim state, the center of which later became Damascus.

The Ottoman Village houses

Pella or as known in Arabic Tabaqat Fahl, is one of the richest archaeological sites in Jordan. the historical data here extends from the Neolithic periods; some of the oldest settlements were found here, and in the classical era Pella was a member of the Decapolis cities under Rome. Although the remains discovered here are not massive, but the traditional classical structure is obvious.

Remains Of the Byzantine church

The site has been busy through different periods due to the all time running stream through the valley towards The Jordan. An ancient

Neolithic temple was discovered on the northern hill which is probably some 10,000 years old with huge stones within its structure, and it is believed that this is one of the oldest in the region.

The ruins of classical PELLA

The place was first mentioned in the Egyptian documents in the 2nd millennium BC, as *Pihil* or *Pihilum*. This was a bustling trade center with connections through Syria, Africa and Cyprus. In the Hellenistic period the name was assimilated into Pella changing position between the Greek states of Ptolemy and the Seleucids. In the Christian era Pella was revived once again and churches were established. It continued to play a role in trade through the region since it is in the vicinity with the West Bank. Many of the artifacts through different eras were retrieved by archaeological surveys showing a continuous inhabitation for almost ten millenniums.

In 634 AD, the Muslim armies met here with the Byzantines on the surrounding hills followed soon after by the Yarmouk battle which ended the rule of Constantinople in the east. The city continued existing through the Muslim period as a rural town and continued to   benefit from trade routes and commerce.

Panorama of Ajloun castle

A short drive to the north-west of Jerash, through pine forests and olive groves will lead you to the castle of Ajloun. Situated on top a hill to the west of the city with the same name, which was originally of a monk who once had his chapel on the spot where the castle is now.

Ajloun is a fine example of the medieval Muslim military architecture; it is dated to the year 1182 and served only for a few years under Saladin, who ordered it to be built by his nephew Izz Addin Usama. The crusade to which the castle is related came to an end after the decisive battle of Hattin opposite Lake Tiberius in 1187.

The strategic location of the hill allows viewing a wide radius of territory and three major gorges surrounding the area; it was necessary for Saladin at the time to prevent any penetration by the crusaders from the west through the Jordan Valley.

The area also was very well known for its contents of iron ore which was necessary for weapons production for the war effort.

In 1812, the discoverer of Petra, John Burckhardt visited the castle and gave description of the site in his documents

The entrance to the castle after the bridge

Saladin

His name is Yoousuf ibn Ayyoub ibn Shadi, and his titles are AL Malik An-naser **Salah Ad-din** Abu'l Muzaffar. Born in 1137-38 from Kurdish origins in Iraq, the **Ayyuobids** are related to his father Ayyoub. Served in the army of Nour Ad-din Zanghi who was the first to mark a victory on the crusaders in 1144, and managed to take back Edessa. Saladin's role in Egypt and Syria in the later years lead to a united system ruling the regions of the Islamic state after long political disputes and fall down. His obsession of taking back Jerusalem from the crusaders lead him to a victory in 1187.

Saladin died at the age of 54 in 1193, and chroniclers mention he left nothing behind even for his funeral, dying as simple as he lived. His legacy is the romance of the period and the virtues of chavallry and sacrifice. In the Arab world his name is still mentioned as **The Liberator of Jerusalem.**

Al Azraq meaning the blue because of its water land areas. It existed on the ancient trade routes from the east and the south exit to The Arabian Peninsula. Now it links the country with Iraq, Kuwait and Saudi Arabia. Naturally it was and still the habitat for many flora and fauna species. Two wild life reserves are functioning in the area. The eastern desert of Jordan is a mix of flat landscapes with ancient volcanic rubble scattered around the area, and in some areas volcanic tunnels spread under the desert for miles.

The castle is in the Azraq Ash-shimali town on the junction to Baghdad. Built by the Romans in the 2nd century in a typical Roman fort shape with rough basalt stones.

The entrance to the castle

The area contains also evidence of Nabataean activity, not surprising for the fact of their dominance over the area before Rome. Further surveys over the area show ancient Nabataean dam structures around the valleys, indicating the need for water through the desert to supply the busy road and for irrigation.

The north section of the castle

Two ton basalt door

After annexing Petra, the Romans took over these stations and guarded the area as the last line before Persia.

Exhibits in the castle

The castle was used in later periods, and the story of Lawrence of Arabia also involves this castle with the events at the turn of the 20th century.

Amra bath complex is a UNESCO site that comprises one of the earliest examples of Islamic architecture of the 8th century. It is well known for its frescos depicted in the vaults inside the building, especially the zodiac in the dome of the calidarium. Seemingly this was a relaxation and bathing spot for the emirs and elite of the Umayyad state. The nearby ruins on the north side may indicate there was a compound, maybe a palace remains leveled to the ground by earthquakes.

The Amra Bath complex

The place was restored through many years and most of the frescos are visible after years of fire and graffiti. It is believed that the Greek artists did the interior decoration with mosaics and frescos, showing different themes from other cultures and some related to the ruling caliph of Damascus showing him in a victorious theme over the rest of the rulers around the Islamic state.

Some of the frescos contain earthly paradise impressions of lush gardens, naked women, cupid, vine, hunters and animals. Contradicting with the principles of Islam where iconography is forbidden in any manner, this site is considered an exception knowing the landlord; this was the time of Al Waleed bin Abdulmalik bin Marwan, who is told to have been not very committed to Islamic conducts.

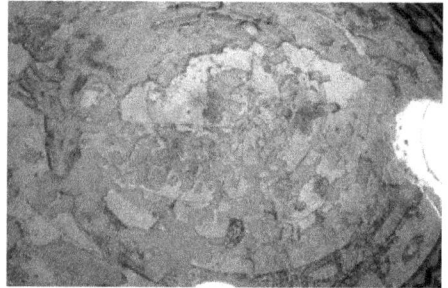

The Calidarium dome with the zodiac in frescos

This is the most preserved of the Umayyad Islamic period in Jordan. Some 15 minutes drive to the west from Amra Baths contained in the same natural landscape. It is mentioned that this was a meeting place of the Umayyads with local tribes. The inside of the castle-like palace is more lucrative than it seems in the beginning. It is a combination of two floors of dining and guest rooms in the second and stables and service rooms in the lower.

Examining the facility from inside will reveal the deceptive outside look. There is a small courtyard in the center surrounded with rooms and sections almost replicated from either side. Stairways through narrow passages lead to the upper floors to the fine stucco decorated dining rooms, all this was done using the material available in the area. The style is very similar to the tradional mud houses with stone cladding, and probably there were additions in the mortar used to make it more lasting.

The interior of a dining room

Regardless of numerous earthquakes through centuries; this structure is still in a remarkable shape, and it is one of the most atmospheric and beautiful buildings of ancient Jordan.

The stucco details

Madaba is the mosaics center in Jordan; ancient and new. It is well known for the Church of St. George in the center of the town. The Mosaic Map of The Hoy Land contained in this church is the main attraction of the city, although there are hundreds of mosaics and archaeological spots within the city combined in what is called The Archaeological Park of Madaba.

A fragment of the Map showing Jerusalem

The church was built around the year 560 AD, in the time of Justinian. It was located on the north gate of the city on the Kings Highway passing through it. This was as a road map for the travelers and pilgrims passing through Transjordan, and places of Christian interest are around the area like Mkawer or Biblical Macheros where according to the Biblical geography John the Baptist was beheaded by the son of Herod. And five miles to the west there is Mt. Nebo, a major point on tourist itineraries around the Dead Sea and Amman.

The existing remains of the map are a part of is believed to have been the depiction of the properties of Byzantium including the north of Africa and the south of Europe. The main focus of the composition is The Holy Land and Jerusalem. This is considered as the first attempt in history to describe geography through mosaics, and only buildings of such character could afford this elaborate kind of art which was very popular at the time.

For the Biblical archaeology this map has been a great source of information about some of the sites of extreme value; like the Baptism site of the Jordan discovered in 1995.

Many of the common Biblical events are described here with the towns and metropolises of the era, many of which still exist.

The church of St. George's

The mosaic depiction of the ancient cities of Rome, Grigoria and Madaba
- The Archaeological Park.

In Deuteronomy 34 describing Moses at the end of his journey, Nebo was the place where the prophet lived his last moments. The Old Testament mentions the land of Moab as the final rest place of Moses, and that his burial place is not known.

The early Christians decided that this was the spot with the view to the Holy Land that fits the description in Deuteronomy.

In those days pilgrims used to cross the Jordan from Jerusalem through the Livias road linking with the Kings Way near Madaba. In the year 384 AD, a group of pilgrims visited Nebo, it was as mentioned in the chronicles the church of Moses. Egeria, a pilgrim from spain within the group was impressed and spread the word through Europe within the recently established Christian state in Constantinopolis.

The church of Moses

Nebo was restored starting from 1933 by The Franciscans Custody of The Holy Land, and is still sponsored by them and other organizations worldwide. This may be the third or second visited place in Jordan after Petra, and is one of the Christian pilgrimage sites in Jordan.

In an older —than the Bible- historical text on a basalt stele, Nebo is mentioned by *Mesha,* the king of ancient Moab. This stele is now in the Louvre in Paris and recognized as the oldest text found in Jordan and the only outside the Bible mentioning the name *Yahweh.*

THE BAPTISM ON THE JORDAN

This is the greatest archaeological discovery in Jordan at the end of the 20th century. Surveys proved that the area was a passage to the east of Jordan linking with the trade routes, and in the Christian era it was associated with the event of the Baptism of Jesus Christ according to the Biblical texts. All the clues, chronicles and described Biblical geography refer to what was known as the wilderness, the place where John The Baptist lived and baptized people; and that's on the eastern bank of The Jordan.

The Prophet Elijah's hill, some scholars mark this spot as Bethany

The Bible mentions Bethany and Bethabara in different spots, and both apply to the area where remains of different described places where discovered and restored as possible. The site was under meters of soil, chalk and pebble layers and the first serious discoveries of churches and baptistery pools were in 1996.

In the year 2000, the Vatican was the first to officially recognize the new discovery, and celebrations of the third millennium were held here.

The Spring of John The Baptist>

As the Great Rift Valley passes through forming the natural boundary between The Holy Land and Transjordan, it is the lowest point on earth- 400 meters below sea level, and is one of the saltiest waters on the planet. With no outlets to the open sea these waters trap all the minerals contained in the surrounding layers pouring in by The Jordan and seasonal rain water flow.

In the Biblical texts it is called The Sea of Salt, and in the Muslim traditions this is the place where the cities of Sodom and Gomorrah once existed; it is called The Sea of Lot.

In ancient times The Dead Sea was the source of bitumen and minerals used in sacred burial rituals by the existing here cultures. There is no life in these waters except three kinds of bacteria that depend on each other to exist; and that's where the sweet waters mix with the salty waters. About 33% of the water is salt and minerals, Magnesium chloride is half the mineral content. Eventually, this composition makes it ten times saltier than The Mediterranean. For the Jordanian economy potash industry is the second source of income after the phosphates.

The Dead Sea is a favorite as a relaxation area for locals and visitors alike, and it's an all year round resort area with a good infrastructure of hotels, beaches and resorts.

Ecologically, the level of water is reducing; and that's due to the diversion of The Jordan waters to the south of Israel in the Negev desert for irrigation; the result is more evaporation than incoming water, and the level of the water bed goes down by one meter every year. In its original size the water bed was some 80 km long and 25 wide, now it is around 65 by 20 km divided into two separated areas.

The bottom of the Dead Sea is totally white of around 3 km thick salt layers 400 meters below the surface.

According to this, the Jordan Valley and The Dead Sea form the subtropical climate conditions in the country and provide a natural habitat for many species of flora and fauna, like the Dead Sea Sparrow that lives only here. Many of these species are protected by establishing natural protected areas and reserves to maintain the numbers and health of the endangered animals like the Caracal and the ibex.

Karak represents one of the ancient Moabite strongholds, it is mentioned in the Bible as Kir Heres, and the crusaders called it Le krak du Moab. Situated in the central part of Jordan opposite the Dead Sea of the Sharah mountain range, it controls a large section of the Kings Way passing to the east from it. The place is known for its medieval era castle built by the occident in 1139-1142, after being concentrated in Shobak Mountains as a stronghold in *Oultrejordan* or Tranjordan.

A chain of castles stretched from the Red Sea to Antioch during the First Crusade and the territory of Jordan contains some of them. And this is the biggest of them. Situated on the south of citadel and protected by efficient high walls and towers. This castle was a serious threat to the efforts of Saladin to liberate the occupied lands and establish one system in Syria and Egypt. Major routes of caravans and pilgrims to Mecca passed through the nearby Kings Way and parallel routes that were in the range of the castle, and through decades of its activity many attacks were held against these routes and caravans, and the connections between Cairo and Damascus were disrupted in many occasions. Eventually, the castle became the first target of Saladin's armies in Transjordan.

The original entrance to the castle

The Muslim armies tried more than once to take over the place, but with no significant success. The castle was invincible and well planed, and Saladin was able to seize it by starving the opponent out through several months of siege. The fall of the castle was in 1187, after the defeat in Hattin in the north of Palestine.

In later periods the castle was used by the Ayyoubids followed by the Mamluks who added to its structure and enhanced its fortifications. In the Ottoman period this was a stronghold for rather small garrisons or was used as a prison for the convicted. In the later days the Ottomans destroyed parts of it to prevent it to be used against them by the locals.

A fragment of arabesque ornament in the castle

Le krak du Mont Real was the Frankish name of this panoramic stronghold; probably this is one of the most scenic spots of Jordan. Situated on a conical and difficult to climb hill top the castle controlled the area with the roads stretching further to Arabia and Egypt.

It is mentioned that this castle was established in 1115, as the first stronghold of he crusades in Transjordan, and after almost three dacedes the center was moved to Karak because of its vicinity to Jerusalem and the direct visual contact range to it through the Dead Sea.

Here you will see the traditional military architecture of the era that left significant effect on the peoples of the region and Europe together. Amd like the rest of such facilities, they were reused in later times and additions were made to it; and the same damage was made to it by the Ottoman rulers to paralyze any possible mutiny by the tribes living here.

One of the Muslim era towers on the east walls

The inside halls of the castle

A view from the west of the castle

PETRA

The most fascinating site in Jordan; the rose red city of the desert or Metropolis Arabia as the Romans called it after annexing it to their land in the beginning of the 2nd C.

Situated in the south within the Sharah Mountains, formed by millions of years of geological activity under the sea waters; sedimentary layers of sand were compressed and later formed by erosion after being exposed to wind, rain and side rivers. The unusual shapes of these mountains are characteristic; the amazing colors of the rock vary in different times of the day.

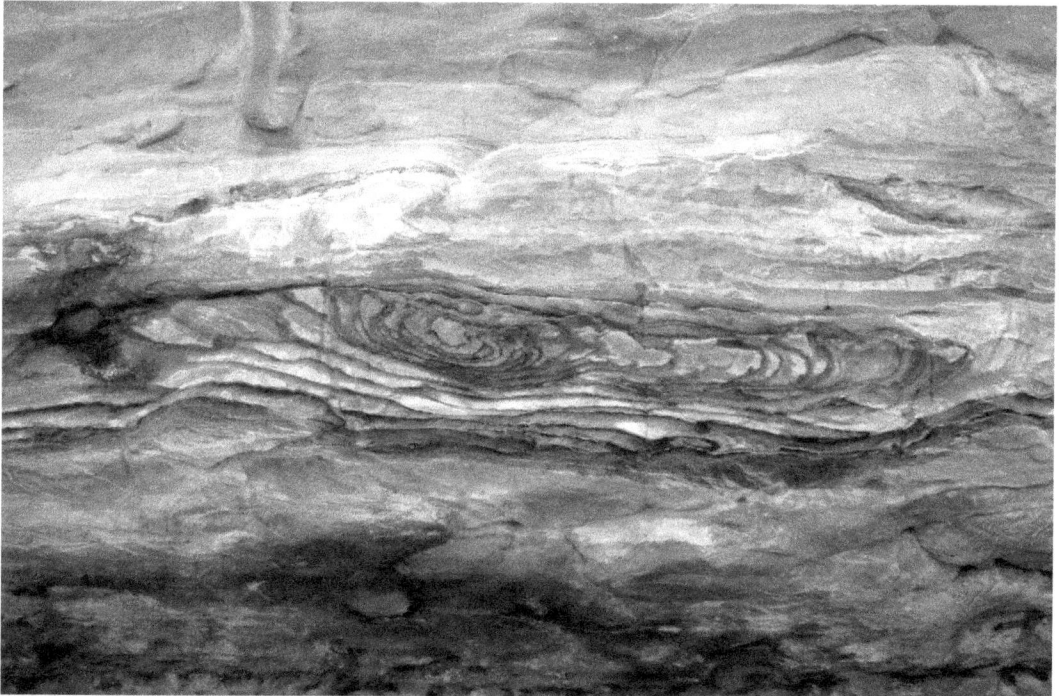

Colored rocks

Petra is to the west of Wadi Mousa-the Valley of Moses-; a town settled by the local Bedouin tribes living here since centuries.

Historically the place was mentioned in the Old Testament as parts of the ancient Kingdom of Edom; though which Moses is believed to have passed with his people during the Exodus from Egypt; and buried his brother Aaron on top of a mountain in the west of the site; now this is one of the tracks through the site. To see the ruins some five days are needed; this is the biggest archaeological site in the country.

Excavations are still being held frequently by numerous institutes. Petra was enlisted in the UNESCO World Heritage sites list in 1986.

The story of the Nabataean city begins with a forced migration in the 7th C. BC, from the territory of Yemen as many historians believe. Those tribes used to call themselves Nabtu; which means the stone masters in Arabic. The Greek name Petra is taken from its natural description which is the rocks, while the Nabataeans called it Reqem or Sela' bearing the same meaning. Old historical chronicles mention that the city started to be formed by the 4th C. BC, as an organized metropolis hidden within the mountains for security; since the area was surrounded by rough sandstone with very few entrances through except the gorge or the Siq as locally called; this is a mile long serpent passage to the ancient city that provided a secure —easy to defend- gate.

When established here, Petra started to play a major role in the regional trade; the Nabataeans overtook the control on the connections between different parts of the region; eventually becoming the merchants of goods transported from remote parts of the ancient world.

The Tomb of Aaron

The city enjoyed a good position in the region until it was folded under the Roman rule by Trajan, who started establishing roads and highways through the south of Syria, and the Kings Highway is one of his major achievements. The consequences of such an act were devastating for the people of Petra; the trade routes were shifted further to the north closer to Damascus, and its residents started to abandon it gradually settling in the northern parts of Jordan and moving their capital city to Damascus and Bosra in the south of Syria. in the later centuries Petra was forgotten except for a few communities that lived here until the midst of the 8th C.

The central street in Petra with the view of the Great Temple

In those days Petra formed the center of the Nabataean Kingdom that stretched from the north of Saudi Arabia up to Damascus, and from the borders of Iraq to Sinai. The Roman Empire was the outer force that brought to an end a whole community of tribes ruled by a monarchy for almost a millennium. With the change of powers, this becomes one of the Christian cities in the south of Jordan, churches were established here and later this became a bishopric seat until the 7th C.

In the new era Petra was rediscovered by John Burckhardt, a Swiss traveler who passed through in 1812 after visiting the north of Jordan.

Since then, archaeological expeditions started to flow in, and with the rise of the new state of Jordan the site was developed and excavated with the help of different museums and organizations from around the world.

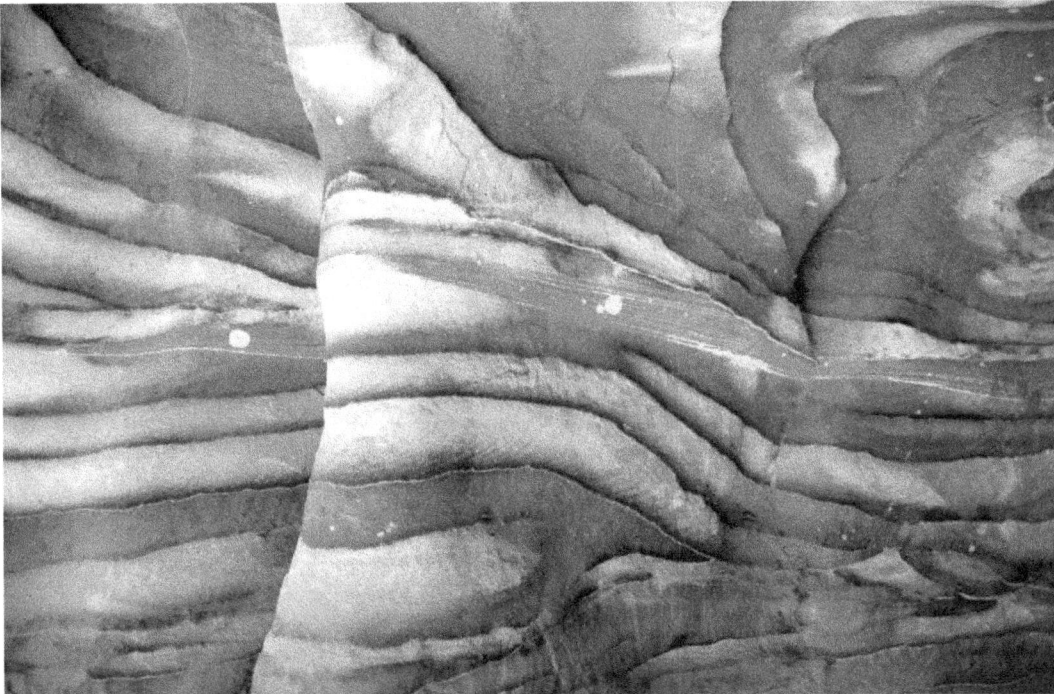

Colored rocks

Scholars mention that less than 20% of the history of this kingdom is revealed. Many sites outside Petra are yet to be studied and excavated and there is hope that more information will surface in the future about this amazing nation that established one of its kind city in such harsh conditions of the desert.

Many of the genius solutions for water and aqueducts were revealed here, and in some sections the water systems still function with reservoirs and pools that are still being used by the locals for their needs. There are even studies being conducted to understand the systems laid some 2000 years ago.

The entrance to the site starts from the end of the town of Wadi Mousa through the valley extending to the west. From the gateway there is some half a mile before the gorge leading into the city.

On the way to the gorge, the entrance to Petra

This is a natural water passage descending from the eastern mountains and passing through all the way to the Araba Valley.

As you start walking some of the objects will be on both sides of the river bed marking the first objects and tombs outside the city, but the most impressing is the Obelisque Tomb on the left side just before the curve leading to the gorge or the Siq. It is believed that this was an elite burial facility of the 1st C. AD, an inscription was found on the opoosite side mentioning the name Abdumalku, and it seems there were four people buried here. The upper hall is thought to have been the burial place, and the lower section was traditionally used for memorial rituals connected to the buried people. The chronicles of the classical era mention such rituals like Josephus Flavius, Strabo and Theodore the Sicilian.

The Obelisque Tomb

The gorge itself is originally a crack in the mountain caused by earthquakes and erosion. The Nabataeans chiseled some of the sections in it especially at the entrance and the pavement; traces of instruments are clearly visible everywhere you look round. Another thing you will never miss is the water system stretching all the way down to the city; this was rain and spring water driven to the metropolis for drinking and irrigation.

Although some classical era historians mentioned the Nabataeans as non farming community; the clues to an advanced knowledge in agricultural techniques are clear. The city was decorated with gardens in the open areas inside, and growing products was an essential occupation since this was a city of 40,000 residents during the peak of Petra; for those days this considered a high figure for standard cases, but Petra was is an exception knowing it was a major trade center of the ancient world. The scale of the city is really impressing, and a trip inside would normally take a few hours, in some cases certain tracks consume the whole day especially if you decide to hike to Aaron's Tomb or do the south trail leading to the farthest ruins like Wadi Sabra.

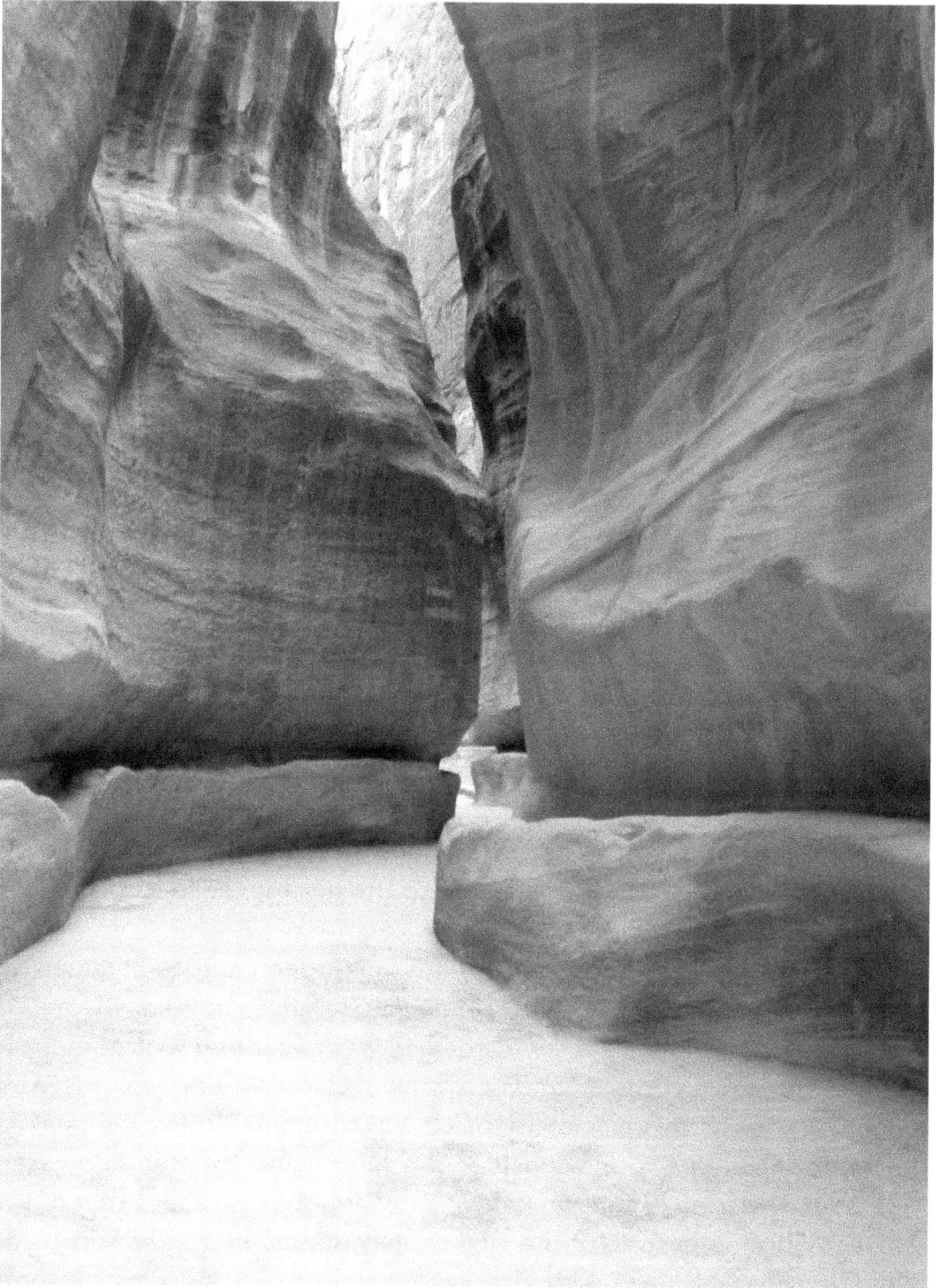

The Siq, gateway to Petra

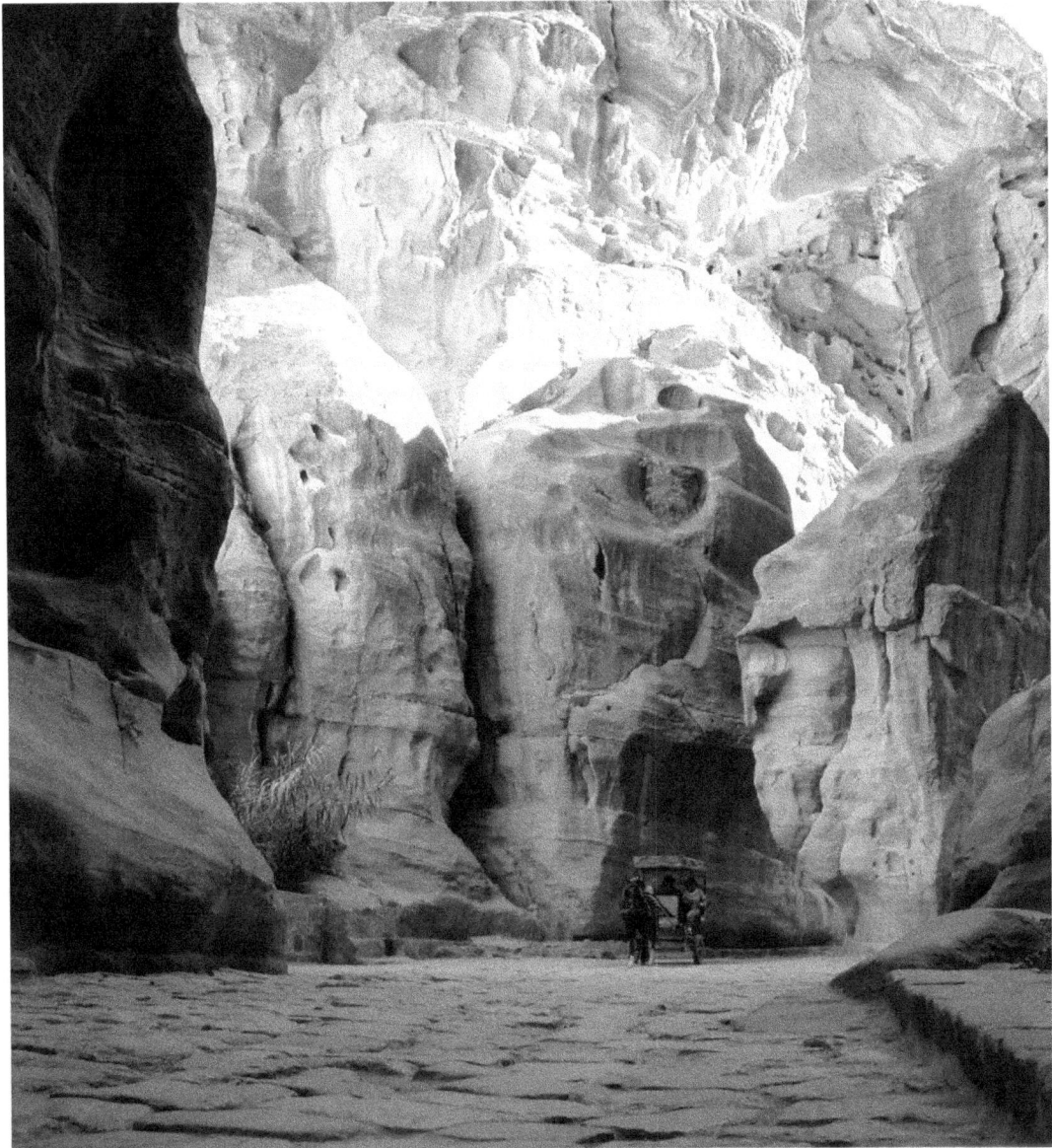

The walk through the Siq is an experience by itself; here you will get close to the extraordinary atmosphere of reddish color, light and shade mixture in these sandstone formations.

The Siq contains many of the symbols left by the Nabataeans; the niches you will see along the passage are of religious and and memorial value, a combination of different beliefs under different names repeating the same lines of the common religions in the region; the Great Mother and the synonym of Zeus or the Roman Jupiter as Dushara here.

The Nabataeans had their religious cults originally from Arabia, but the income of Hellenism made its influence of the peoples of the region, Petra was no exeption. Since the main mythological figures worshipped in Asia or Europe or even Africa were the same, the acceptance of each other's values possibly was not violating the religious sense in those communities, and that's reflected in the best way on the façade of the Treasury, or Khaznat Far'on as it is locally called by the Bedouin tribes who settled here a few centuries ago.

A view of the Treasury from the north

The Treasury of Pharaoh

This is the prize for visitors after the mile walk from the start. This façade is the most beautiful in Petra and the historical symbol of Jordan. Standing 39 meters high and consisting of two levels, this composition is a reflection of the myths concerning life and death, the connection between mortality and immortality.

It is well known that chiseling the rocks initiated from the top of the façade downwards; this is probably the only way in which accuracy and symmetry is acquired. Scholars mention that the Treasury was done in the 1st C. BC, in the place originally where previous burials were existing in a smaller scale. These burials were blocked and hidden under the new elaborate façade.

The motives here are connected to what's called the cycle of life and death, the transition between the two stages and the journey to the fertile heaven with the company of deities related to it; Isis, the Amazonians and religious symbols of fertility; which is eventually the concept of the Great Mother or Mother of Nature. Idol and ancestors worshipping was common in those days and Petra is a fine example of that; the tradition of commemorating the death of their people is obvious in the burials and tombs; usually there would be a funerary hall at the lower section of the burial or on the side depending on the plan and location of the façade. The elite had their specific locations in the most important spots of the city.

Inside a funeral hall opposite the Soldiers Tomb

The central street

The monuments of Petra are mostly concentrated around the central street splitting the city into north and south. The seasonal river bed continues its course through and exits further to the west merging with the Araba Valley on the western borders of Jordan.

Burial Facades- the necropolis of Petra

The theater of Petra

The Royal Tombs over looking the central street

In 2007 Petra was rated as the second in the New Seven Wonders of the world, even before this occasion the city was called the Eighth Wonder. It still can surprise us with its history and landmarks, recent excavations by The Brown University revealed what is called The Great Temple in the central colonnaded street. Others call it The Elephants Temple; because of the decorated crowns of the columns in this elegant building that was wrecked by earthquakes.

A fragment of the columns with an elephant head

The Great Temple

Qasr Al Bint- Palace of Pharaoh's Daughter- temple

By the end of the central street, the track leads to the main temple of Petra. One of the few built structures that survived centuries of erosion and seismic activity; wooden beams were fixed in the walls to reduce the effect of earthquakes, seemingly it worked, but the roof didn't hold up.

The Hellenistic style is visible here like in the Treasury and many other buildings and facades in the city. Stucco with decorative motives is still on parts of the walls, some sources mention this place also as an archive for the city because of the thick walls embracing the building to prevent humidity inside the temple.

This is yet another case where the local tribes related similar structures to the pharaohs of Egypt; and that comes from the belief that the pharaoh was also here while chasing Moses and his people, in addition to that the pharaohs and legends of Egypt were well known, and it was easier making them responsible for these creations. These ideas -as told by the locals- were the reason for an endless treasure hunt around the area, and the Treasury itself suffered from this at some point.

The façade of the Monastery- Ad Deir- the second face of Petra

The most significant after the Treasury and the other face of the coin, the Monastery or Ad Deir in Arabic is a remote spot on top of the mountains to the north-west from the end of the center, it's about two miles of an ascending track facing the Wadi Araba Valley.

It is mentioned in different history sources that this was a worshipping place for the Nabataeans facing the desert before Ghaza and Sinai; these were some of the important ancient trade routes they used to deliver their merchandize to the awaiting ports and destinations around the region were they also had their station towns and stopover points.

The traditional location and atmosphere of such facilities is present here; the higher, the closer to Gods.

The breathtaking panorama available in front of the Monastery gives a view to a large section of the valley beyond, and looking slightly to the south from here the Tomb of Aaron stands on the highest peak in these sandstone mountains. This is where the city ends practically there is no other easier way to go back than the same track connecting it to the center of the metropolis.

LITTLE PETRA

A few kilometers to the north from the town of Wadi Mousa the famous location of the caravan service town is located in the northern mountains of Petra. Different sources mention this place as the base for the caravans used by the Nabataeans, and some mention it was an elite neighborhood of Petra; remains of elaborate mantions were discovered here recently indicating the rich life style conducted here.

Supposed traces of residential and service compounds are around the area, and one of the most famous sites of the Neolithic period is here, this is some 10,000 years ago.

The Neolithic village of Al Beida

The classical site of Litle Petra includes tricliniums and service facilities with a sufficient system of aqueducts and reservoirs around the town. One of the facades inside contains a recently restored fresco depicting a scene in paradise with the images of Eros and birds in lush gardens.

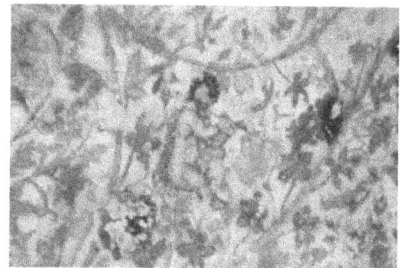

Frescos of Little Petra

WADI RUM

One of the most beautiful deserts in the world and the geological sister of Petra; this was a former sea that declined millions of years ago, and reshaped by side rivers, wind and rain. This desert is twenty million years behind the Arizona Desert.

The rough torn mountains with the sand dunes patched with desert shrubs and camel herds are something like in *One Thousand and One Nights* tales. The quiet atmosphere with the fascinating light and shade effects makes this desert a favorite on the tourist itineraries. T.E. Lawrence of Arabia had his adventures here and the start point for the events at the turn of the 20th century took place on these sands. The famous movie of Lawrence of Arabia was filmed here in 1962. The local Bedouin tribes played a major role in those events and participated in the war effort with the legendary English officer.

Now Wadi Rum is a natural reserve protected by the government in hope to protect and restore the previous conditions of he wild life endangered by overhunting and the growth of local towns and villages.

Historically, the place was a inhabited by ancient tribes ho left traces of their culture in the manner of wall drawings with pictures of animals and hunting scenes, this was some 4000 years ago according to historical sources.

Drawings on the rocks

A bird eye view of Wadi Rum

In Jordan people call Petra, Wadi Rum and Aqaba the Golden Triangle for their vicinity to each other and for the regular tours held through the mentioned destinations.

Wadi Rum at sunset

The amazing contrasts of the desert

AQABA

In the Biblical texts this junction was the passage for Moses from Sinai to the Land of Edom and further to the north through the Kings Way; it is Ezion Geber of the Old Testament. In the classical period I was called Ayla. This is the Roman Kings Way *—or Via Nova Trajana-* endpoint starting from the south of Damascus. The name Aqaba means the junction and was used in the Islamic period.

As in the rest of Jordan, Stone and Bronze Age settlements were discovered here, while most of the classical Nabataean and Roman towns were discovered under the modern city buildings.

This served as a vital passage for trade routes connecting the north of Sinai with the west of Asia and Arabia, and also as a strategic connection for the Roman army to circle around the Arabian Peninsula in case of confrontation with Persia. It still continues to play an important role in the Jordanian economy as the only exit to the open sea; most of the commercial activity is involved with Aqaba, as well as tourist itineraries joining several countries of the region together.

Aqaba is a year round resort for both locals and visitors, and is a good choice to start exploring the south of Jordan. The rich marine life existing in these waters makes it a favorite place for diving and snorkeling in addition to water sports activities. It is said that around 20% of the marine life of the Red Sea is concentrated in this gulf with some of the finest coral reefs.

A view of the city

Remains of Islamic Ayla

Islamic Ayla

In some historical sources Aqaba hosted one of the oldest churches in the world, and the first medieval era castle, the traces of which have disappeared due to continuous inhabitation and remodeling the city.

At the turn of the twentieth century this was a usual fishing town and a Turkish post at the Red Sea, and here was the first spark of the Arab Revolt raised against the Ottoman rule during the events of WW1.

As mentioned in the chronicles of those days the castle of Aqaba was sacked by Lawrence and his companions of fifty men after a dangerous three days trip through the desert in order to attack it from the east were no guns were pointed at.

At the entrance to the castle of Aqaba

This castle is believed to have been reestablished in the 15th C, on the ruins of similar former facilities, the crusader castle may have been standing here in the 12th C. now it is known in the history of modern Jordan as the first residence of King Abdullah I son of the Hashemite Sharif Husain bin Ali, the direct descendant of the Prophet Muhammad's dynasty and the great grandfather of the now ruling king Abdullah bin Al Husain II.

Acknowledgments

Special thanks to:

Basheer Daoud: photo

p. 47, 52, 56 bottom,65, 66 bottom.

Denis Kuritsin: photo

p. 54.

Luis Dingley: photo

p. 12 top.

JTB (Jordan Tourism Board): photo

p. 5 map, 6 bottom, 13, 34 top, 39.

ASEZA (Aqaba Special Economic Zone Authority) : photo

p. 69 top left.

RSCN (The Royal Society for the Conservation of Nature) : photo

p. 2, 23, 68.

And to all who helped providing material for this book.